Contents

Weblink: www.curriculumvisions.com

What are microbes?

Microbes are living things that can only be seen with the help of a microscope.

MICRO-ORGANISMS, or **MICROBES**, were the very first living things. They first lived three billion years ago. They are still the most common form of living thing in the world.

Microbes are invisible unless you look through a powerful **MICROSCOPE** (Picture 1). In fact, people have only known about microbes since 1673. This was the year the microscope was invented.

The importance of microbes

Everything you see – the pages of this book, your fingers, your teeth, your food – is covered with microbes. A single teaspoon of soil contains over 1,000,000,000 **BACTERIA**, about 120,000 **FUNGI** and 25,000 **ALGAE**. If all the microbes living on the Earth could be gathered in one place, they would take up more space than all the world's animals!

▼ **(Picture 1) Microbes are living things too small to be seen. The word covers a wide range of tiny living things.**

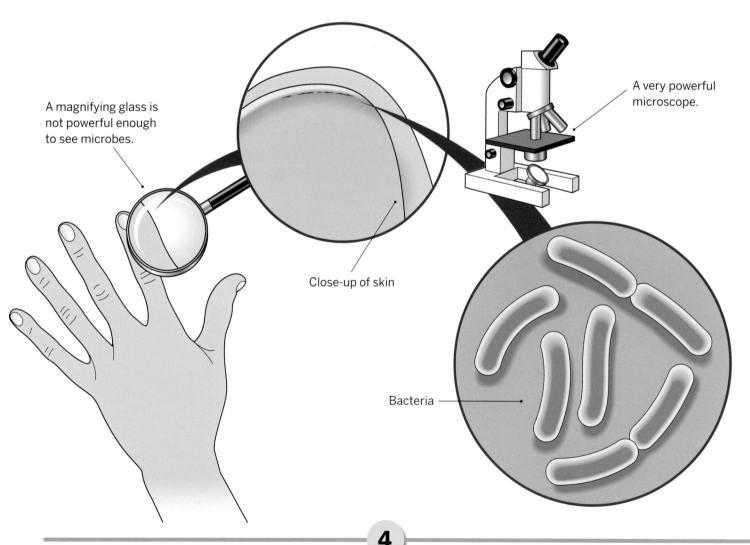

A magnifying glass is not powerful enough to see microbes.

A very powerful microscope.

Close-up of skin

Bacteria

Weblink: www.curriculumvisions.com

Microbes

A brief history

TODAY... 1950s The first mass vaccinations begin to protect children against a range of diseases. This programme will be responsible for saving millions of lives... 1953 Jonas Salk invents the first effective polio vaccine... 1928 Sir Alexander Fleming invents the first antibiotic. It is called penicillin... 1910 Paul Erlich invents chemotherapy, the technique of using chemicals to kill microbes that cause disease but leave the other parts of the body unharmed... 1905 Robert Kock gets the Nobel prize for identifying the organism responsible for tuberculosis... 1885 In France, Louis Pasteur develops a vaccine to protect against the disease called rabies... 1865 Joseph Lister finds that microbes can cause infections in wounds, including those made during surgery. He uses carbolic acid during surgery in hospital to clean the wounds and cut down on infections... 1796 In England, Edward Jenner takes some fluid from the puss caused by cowpox and transfers it from a dairymaid to a young boy by making an injection. This is the first successful vaccination and it protects the boy from smallpox... 1673 Anton van Leeuwenhoek in Holland is the first person to see a microbe. He does this using a microscope he has built himself... 3 billion years ago – microbes are the earliest forms of life on the Earth. They are similar to the algae we find today...

For more information visit www.curriculumvisions.com

Word list

These are some science words that you should look out for as you go through the book. They are shown using CAPITAL letters.

ALGA (plural **ALGAE**)
Tiny, plant-like living things, usually freely floating. Algae have a green colouring and get energy from sunlight.

ANTIBIOTIC
A chemical substance produced by a microbe that kills other microbes.

BACTERIUM (plural **BACTERIA**)
A tiny, one-celled creature. Some give important benefits to people, while others are the main cause of infectious disease.

CELL
The basic unit of all living things. Most microbes are made of just one cell.

DIARRHOEA
Very rapid movement of food through our insides. As a result, it comes out in a very watery form.

DISEASE
A general word for an illness. However, the most common kind of diseases are those caught as a result of invasion by microbes.

ENERGY
The ability to do work.

FOOD POISONING
An illness brought about when food that contains a large number of bacteria is eaten. The bacteria release poisons as they break down the food.

FUNGUS (plural **FUNGI**)
Usually a tiny, plant-like creature that lacks the green colouring of true plants and so is often white or grey.

GERM
Any microbe that causes disease.

IMMUNISE
To protect against severe infection by giving a weakened dose of the infection.

INFECTION, INFECTIOUS DISEASE
An invasion of the body by microbes. If the microbes cause illness as a result, it is called an infectious disease.

MEDICINE
A chemical (drug) designed to help you get over some kinds of illness.

MICRO-ORGANISM
The long word for living things that can only be seen with the aid of a microscope.

MICROBE
A shortened word for micro-organism.

MICROSCOPE
An instrument for looking at very small things.

PARASITE
A living thing that gets its food by living off another living thing.

PLANKTON
Microbes that float about in oceans, rivers and lakes.

PROTOZOAN (plural **PROTOZOA**)
Tiny, animal-like creatures. They are larger than bacteria and often eat bacteria.

VIRUS
The smallest of the microbes and so simple that it is not truly a living thing on its own. It can only live in the cells of other living things.

Weblink: www.curriculumvisions.com

(Picture 2) This water is green because it contains millions of tiny microbes called algae. They are not harmful in themselves, but they are an indication that the water is becoming stagnant and might therefore contain many other unseen but harmful microbes too.

You may not be able to see microbes without a microscope, but you have certainly been affected by what they do. In fact, without microbes all plants and animals could not live.

Microbes are responsible for, among many other things, digesting your food, the rising of dough, the fermenting of wine and beer, the flavour of cheese, the green colour of stagnant water (Picture 2), the flu, the common cold and really terrifying diseases such as smallpox, polio, tuberculosis and Aids.

As you can see, microbes can be responsible for good things and bad. Most of them are good for us, or do nothing. Very few are bad for us. We have a special name for disease-producing microbes – **GERMS**. But, as we have said, most microbes are good for us, so it is unwise to try to get rid of all microbes!

What do microbes look like?

A microbe looks like nothing else on Earth. It doesn't look like any plant or any animal. Microbes sometimes behave a bit like plants (some can make their own food) and a bit like animals (some microbes eat others).

Microbes are very simple creatures. Even the biggest are made of just a single **CELL**, usually less than one tenth of a millimetre across.

Microbes have a skin-like wall that surrounds them. Inside this wall is a fluid, and in the fluid are the substances needed for life. Many cells also have long tails which spin like propellers and move the cells about.

Grouping microbes

Although microbes come in many shapes and sizes, they all fit into one of five main groups: bacteria, **VIRUSES**, fungi, algae and **PROTOZOA**. What microbes look like, and what they do, is described in the rest of this book.

Q Can you name a good thing that microbes do for us?

Summary
- Microbes are too small to be seen without a microscope.
- Microbes that cause disease are known as germs.

Weblink: www.curriculumvisions.com

Microbes and your body

Your body is home to trillions of microbes. You would not be able to live without them.

You can't live without microbes. There are trillions of them inside your body and on your skin.

Here is how to find some of the microbes that call your body home. Run your tongue over your teeth before you clean them. You should feel a film on your teeth (Picture 1). This is a slime produced by microbes. But they are not just on your teeth – they are on your tongue, the inside of your mouth and all over your skin. Don't worry – they are not going to eat you alive, and many of them are extremely useful.

Slimy teeth

The slimy coating that develops on your teeth is made by bacteria. They make the slimy coating as they eat any food that may be left in your mouth and on your teeth. They especially like sugary substances. However, as they do this, they release an acid which can eat away at your teeth, causing tooth decay. It can also give you bad breath.

The longer you go between teeth brushing, the thicker the film of bacterial slime becomes.

You can never get rid of all of the microbes by brushing your teeth, but you can keep them under control.

Good digestion

Another place where you find microbes is in your gut, the long tube that goes down from your stomach and makes up most of your insides (Picture 2). More microbes live in here than anywhere else in your body. They break down the food you eat and release substances which your body can use for food and **ENERGY**.

If the balance of microbes in your gut changes in some way, you get 'stomach ache', perhaps **DIARRHOEA**, and even a fever, until the balance of microbes gets back to normal.

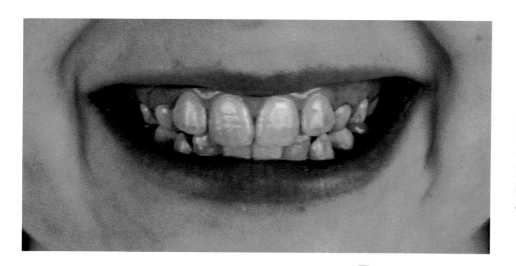

◄ **(Picture 1) This special dentist's dye shows how many bacteria remain on teeth even after they have been cleaned. It is impossible to get rid of all bacteria, but a small number are not harmful.**

6

▶ (Picture 2) How stomach ulcers are caused.

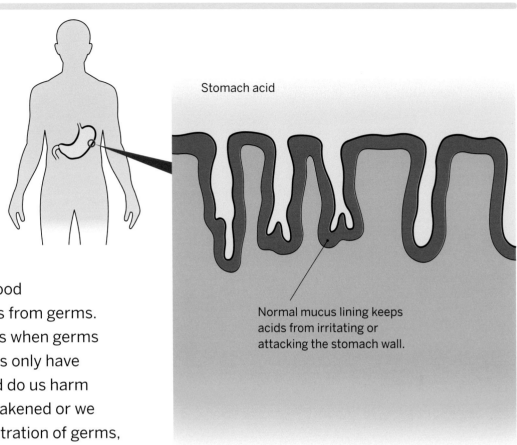

Stomach acid

Normal mucus lining keeps acids from irritating or attacking the stomach wall.

Infection

Normally, the good microbes in our bodies far outnumber the harmful ones (germs) and fight the germs for space. In this way the good microbes help protect us from germs.

An **INFECTION** happens when germs multiply inside us. Germs only have the room to multiply and do us harm if other microbes are weakened or we are exposed to a concentration of germs, such as when someone who has an infection sneezes on us.

Germs can release poisons inside you, or destroy and change your healthy body cells. This makes you feel ill. These kinds of microbes have to be destroyed, and the body normally does this without any help. However, if the infection is too severe, we also use **MEDICINES**.

 Q How do good microbes stop us from becoming ill most of the time?

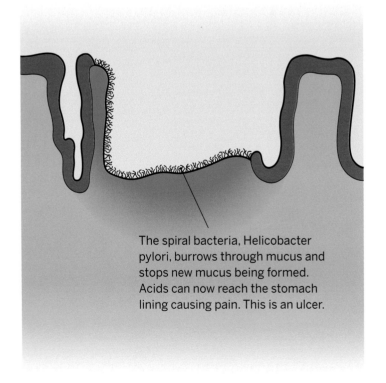

The spiral bacteria, Helicobacter pylori, burrows through mucus and stops new mucus being formed. Acids can now reach the stomach lining causing pain. This is an ulcer.

Summary
- You have microbes inside your body and on your skin.
- Microbes help you to digest your food.
- Microbes on your teeth can cause tooth decay.

Weblink: www.curriculumvisions.com

Bacteria

Bacteria are small microbes that eat and recycle dead matter and turn it into food. Some are also a source of infection.

A bacterium (plural: bacteria) has a single cell surrounded by a thick wall made of a type of sugar. This lets liquid food in and liquid waste out. Many bacteria have a long tail which spins, or thrashes about, and helps them to move.

Bacteria are often no more than one thousandth of a millimetre long (Picture 1).

Bacteria names and shapes

Bacteria come in three common shapes (Picture 2): rods, balls and corkscrews. The rod-shaped ones are called bacillus, the ball-shaped ones are called coccus and the corkscrew ones are called spirillum.

How bacteria live

Some bacteria make their own food from sunlight, or from chemicals found in air, soil or water. However, most bacteria feed on chemicals made by other living things.

▼ **(Picture 1) This is a simple rod-shaped bacterium. Bacteria breed by splitting in two (dividing) when they reach a certain size.**

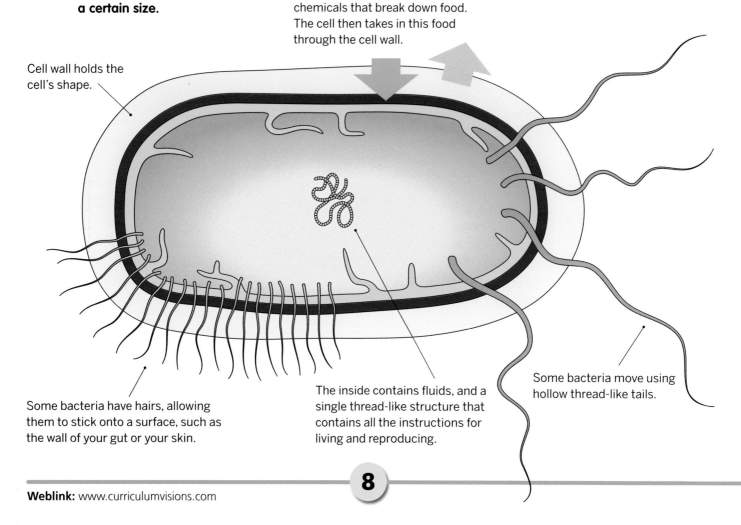

The bacterium produces special chemicals that break down food. The cell then takes in this food through the cell wall.

Cell wall holds the cell's shape.

Some bacteria have hairs, allowing them to stick onto a surface, such as the wall of your gut or your skin.

The inside contains fluids, and a single thread-like structure that contains all the instructions for living and reproducing.

Some bacteria move using hollow thread-like tails.

Weblink: www.curriculumvisions.com

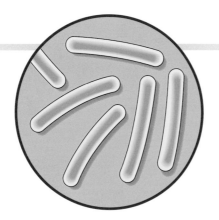

▶ (Picture 2) The three main shapes of bacteria.

Rod-shaped Bacillus bacteria.

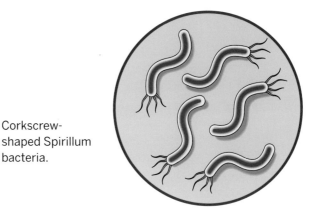

Corkscrew-shaped Spirillum bacteria.

These types of bacteria grow on dead plants and animals, such as the food we eat, or the compost in a garden. They dissolve the dead cells and take out the chemicals they need.

Helpful bacteria

The chemicals that bacteria release as they dissolve dead plants and animals are used as nourishment by other microbes, and by plants and animals. For example, humans have important bacteria in their guts which help to digest food. Bacteria also make certain vitamins your body needs.

Bacteria are particularly important in recycling. For example, they break down human waste in sewage plants.

Harmful bacteria

As you can see, without bacteria, many other living things would not get the nourishment they need to live. But some bacteria also release chemicals that can be harmful, and even cause life-threatening **DISEASE**. Indeed, bacteria are an important cause of **INFECTIOUS DISEASES** in humans.

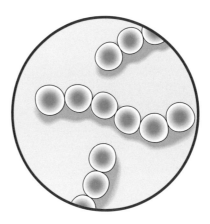

Ball-shaped Streptococcus bacteria.

Occasionally, the bacteria found in foods can cause **FOOD POISONING** in humans. This is one reason why we cook food. For example, pasteurisation (heating food to a high enough temperature to kill the bacteria) is used to kill the bacteria in milk.

Chemicals called antiseptics and germicides are used to kill harmful bacteria on the skin.

Q How do bacteria help in recycling?

Summary
- Bacteria are among the tiniest microbes.
- Bacteria dissolve dead matter and release nourishment.
- Bacteria are a very common source of disease.

Weblink: www.curriculumvisions.com

Fungi

Fungi are thread-like creatures that get their food from plants and animals.

Although **FUNGI** look a bit like plants, they are not plants or animals, but a separate group of living things.

Fungi are more complicated than bacteria. Nevertheless, some fungi, such as the yeast that makes bread dough rise, are very small and are made of only one cell.

A fungus breeds by sending out tiny fruits called spores. Fungi can live for hundreds of years. One species is among the oldest known living things.

There may be as many as 250,000 different kinds (species) of moulds, mildews, rusts, yeasts and mushrooms in the world. All of these are fungi.

Fungi live in the damp

Fungi have no means of producing food for themselves, so they get it from dead plants and animals. This is easiest for them when the remains are damp. Most fungi are found in the damp, warm conditions of the soil. Fungi can also live together with algae. When this happens they form lichen.

Moulds

Moulds have long, branching cells that look like tangled hairs (Pictures 2 and 3). The fuzzy blue, grey and green patches of mould that develop on stale, damp bread are a common example (Picture 1).

▶ **(Picture 1) Mould developing on bread.**

Weblink: www.curriculumvisions.com

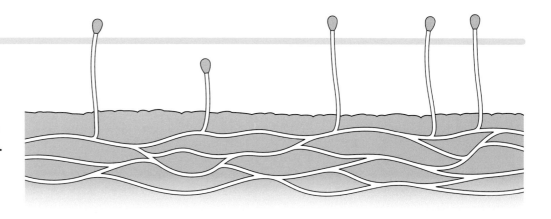

▶ (Picture 2) This is what mould looks like as it grows on bread. It sends out many fibres just below the surface.

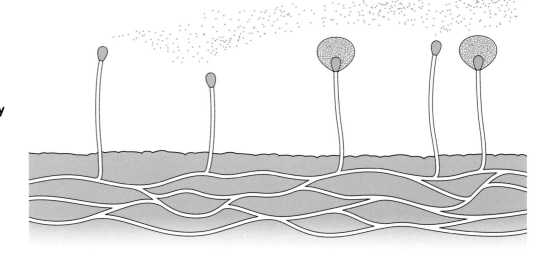

▶ (Picture 3) When the 'fruits' of the fungus burst, they send out a cloud of tiny spores (seeds) which are easily carried by the air.

Helpful and harmful fungi

Fungi can be both harmful and helpful to people. Fungi can also thrive on living tissue. Athlete's foot is an example of a fungus that thrives on humans. There are many others.

Moulds can destroy crops during a damp summer, and they are a cause of food rot (Picture 4). Yet moulds also help break down dead leaves, make humus for soil, help to mature cheese (see also page 16) and they make substances that can be used to prevent disease.

Penicillium is a green mould which stops the growth of bacteria. It was used to make one of the first **ANTIBIOTICS** (called penicillin).

Some fungi are **PARASITES**, which grow on and feed off living things. These are the fungi that mainly cause disease and death. Most commonly, fungi attack plants, but they can also attack animals, including people.

▶ (Picture 4) The rotting part of this lemon is covered with fungi.

Q What conditions do fungi need to survive?

Summary
- Fungi include moulds and yeast.
- Some fungi are useful to us, but others can cause disease.

11

Viruses

5

Viruses are minute creatures that live inside live cells.

Viruses are not at all like the other microbes. A virus is so tiny that it takes the highest-powered microscope just to see them. Viruses range from 20 to 400 thousandths of a millimetre across! The smallest bacterium is larger than the biggest virus.

Viruses are alive but they are not cells. They are just bundles of 'instructions' in a type of skin. They are the simplest of all living things.

How viruses live

Because they are not made of complete cells, viruses can only breed if they can get inside a cell of some other creature. As a result, all viruses are **PARASITES** and can be harmful to other creatures.

Viruses get all of their food and energy from the cell they infect. In the process, they damage the cell and so cause disease. The common cold, flu, chickenpox and Aids are among the many diseases caused by viruses.

▼ **(Picture 1) How a virus works.**

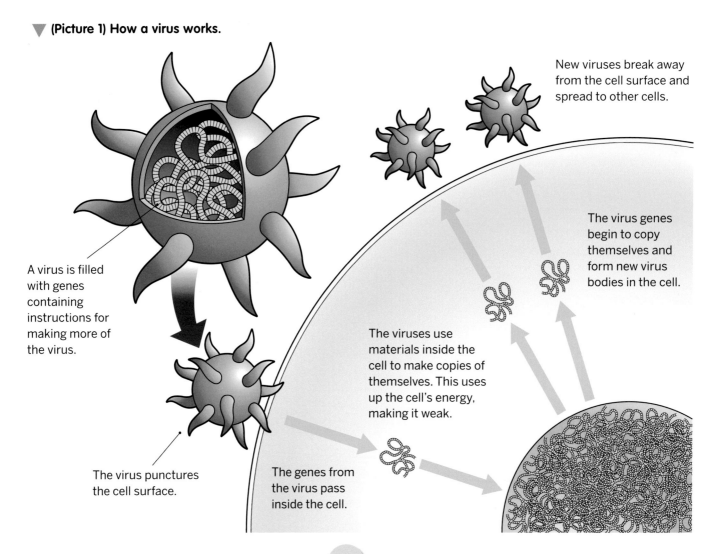

A virus is filled with genes containing instructions for making more of the virus.

The virus punctures the cell surface.

The genes from the virus pass inside the cell.

The viruses use materials inside the cell to make copies of themselves. This uses up the cell's energy, making it weak.

The virus genes begin to copy themselves and form new virus bodies in the cell.

New viruses break away from the cell surface and spread to other cells.

Weblink: www.curriculumvisions.com

Viruses enter through the walls of a cell, breed and produce new copies (Picture 1). These copies then leave through the walls of the cell and enter nearby cells, where the process is repeated.

How viruses behave

Some viruses appear to do no real harm; some kill the cell they live in; others make the cell divide before it dies; yet others cause the cell to grow abnormally. This is what happens with viruses that produce warts.

Depending on what happens, viruses can stay in one area or be carried right around the body.

In many cases a viral infection causes a fever. This is a form of defence, because many viruses stop growing when the body's temperature rises above normal. The body also attacks the virus with a substance called interferon, and makes substances called antibodies that are tailor-made to destroy the virus.

These defences remain in the blood for a long time after the infection and tend to protect the body from being infected again. This is how immunisation works.

Immunisation

To **IMMUNISE** a person against a virus, a weakened or inactivated strain of the virus (called a vaccine) is introduced into the body. This weakened virus does not cause a disease to break out, but it does cause the body to produce antibodies which then protect against any later infection (Picture 2).

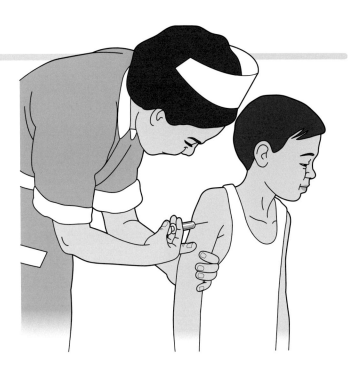

▲ **(Picture 2)** By our taking a vaccine before we are infected by a virus the body 'learns' how to defend against a future infection by that virus before it can cause illness.

Vaccines are mostly taken as an injection of liquid.

Diseases such as measles, mumps, poliomyelitis and rubella are all prevented by immunisation.

Medicines

There are few medicines that can be used directly to combat an infecting virus. This is because viruses stay inside living cells, and any drug that kills the virus will also kill the cells.

How does immunisation work?

Summary
- **Viruses are simple living things that can invade cells.**
- **Viruses can cause disease.**
- **The body makes antibodies to fight viruses.**

Weblink: www.curriculumvisions.com

Microbe plants and animals

Algae are tiny plant-like creatures with a green colouring. They are not harmful and are an important source of food for water-living animals.

There are two groups of microbes that behave more like plants and animals. The plant-like microbes are called algae and the animal-like microbes are called protozoa.

Algae: food and air for the world

Most algae are small green creatures made of a single cell. These algae are bigger than bacteria but even so they cannot be seen without a microscope. They live in fresh and salt, hot or cold water, and they live in the soil and other damp places (Picture 1).

Sometimes huge numbers of algae grow in one place, and then they turn the water green. Green stains on rocks are also a sign of billions of algae concentrated in one place (Picture 2).

All algae use their coloured matter to make food. They use sunlight in just the same way as plants. During this process, algae give out oxygen. It is believed that over half of the world's oxygen supply is made by algae in the oceans.

Some algae have a hard shell. These are called diatoms. You can find them in the slimy rocks by the shore or a rocky river. About three million diatoms can be packed into a teaspoon.

Algae do us no harm and are the food for animals in the sea, just as plants are food for animals on land. Whales, fish, shrimps, clams, and worms are just some of the vast number of creatures that depend upon algae for their food.

About five hundred species of algae are eaten by humans, especially by people in East Asia and the Pacific. Algae is farmed in shallow bays around the coasts of Japan.

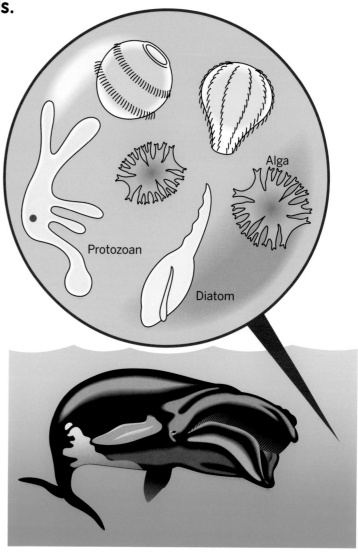

▲ **(Picture 1) Water may look clear but actually contains multitudes of tiny floating plants (algae) and animals (protozoa) called PLANKTON. Whales even use them as food.**

14

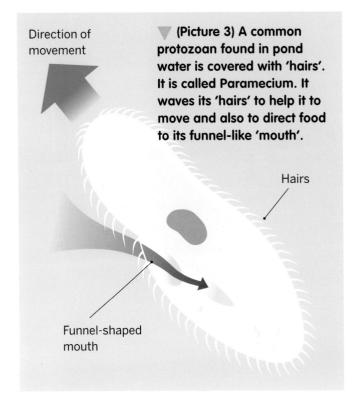

(Picture 2) Sometimes the numbers of algae grow so great that they can be seen coating the surface of rocks, as here in this hot spring. Although you cannot see them because they do not occur in quite such large numbers, algae are also found coating damp soil particles and most other damp surfaces on land.

Direction of movement

(Picture 3) A common protozoan found in pond water is covered with 'hairs'. It is called Paramecium. It waves its 'hairs' to help it to move and also to direct food to its funnel-like 'mouth'.

Hairs

Funnel-shaped mouth

Protozoa: good and bad

Protozoa (which means 'first animal') are single-celled microbes that are in many ways like animals (Picture 3). Most live in water but they are also found in moist soil (where there may be up to 100,000 in a gram of moist soil), and some live in plants and animals. We are home to some protozoa. About a third of protozoa are parasites.

Most protozoa feed on bacteria, algae and small animals. Protozoa are important for the fertility of soils. They 'graze' on old soil bacteria, leaving the soil to contain mostly young bacteria which break down dead plant matter faster than old bacteria do. Protozoa also release nitrogen and phosphorus, which are important fertilisers for plants.

Protozoa are used in waste treatment plants to help break down sewage. The protozoa eat the harmful bacteria in the sewage. Indeed, it is impossible to produce good, clean water without protozoa.

The parasite kinds of protozoa are, however, harmful. They are responsible, for example, for African sleeping sickness and malaria.

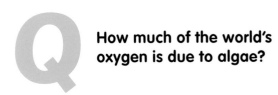

Q How much of the world's oxygen is due to algae?

Summary
- Algae are tiny water-living plant-like creatures.
- Algae produce most of the world's food and oxygen.
- Protozoa are animal-like creatures.
- Algae and protozoa make plankton.

Weblink: www.curriculumvisions.com

Microbes make food

Microbes need to eat, and they eat the same food as us. This can be good news.

We get our nourishment by eating and drinking. But as we take food and drink into our bodies, we are also taking in microbes.

Bread

There are many kinds of bread. Some breads (such as naan bread and tortillas) are flat and dense, whereas loaves of bread and dinner rolls are light. When you look at a loaf of bread you can see the reason for the lightness: it is full of tiny holes (Picture 1). These were made by bubbles of gas that formed during baking.

Bread that rises and makes bubbles is called leavened bread. The bubbles are made by a microbe called yeast, which is a type of fungus.

This is what yeast looks like.

▲ (Picture 1) The holes in this bread are bubbles of carbon dioxide gas made as the yeast 'eats' part of the bread. The bubbles make the bread swell up. This is what we call 'rising'.

Baker's yeast is made of dried-out clumps of this fungus. When yeasts are added to a dough, they eat sugars in the dough and release a gas (carbon dioxide). This happens when you leave dough to rise before baking it. When you bake the bread, you kill the yeast – but the gas makes the bread fluffy. Yeast is also used in making beer and wine (Picture 2).

◀ (Picture 2) This is a picture of a winery. The wine is made by allowing grape juice to be eaten by yeast while it is in large wooden casks. The cloudiness in the jar in the middle of the picture is produced by dead yeast. It will be filtered off to give clear wine.

Weblink: www.curriculumvisions.com

Cheese

Cheese is a curdled form of milk. Curdling separates the curd – cheese – from watery liquids called whey. This is done by bacteria when they release chemicals called enzymes.

The microbes used in cheese-making give cheeses their distinctive flavour. At the same time, the rapid growth of the cheese-making microbes stops the growth of any harmful microbes and preserves the cheese.

Later, salt is added to the curd to bring out the flavour and to preserve the cheese. Microbes cannot grow in salt.

Surface-mould ripened cheeses, such as Brie, and blue-veined cheeses, such as Roquefort, rely on a penicillin fungus (Picture 3).

The holes in some cheeses, such as Gruyere, are made by warming the ripening cheeses for a while, so that bacteria grow and release carbon dioxide gas which forms bubbles in the cheese. The cheese is then moved back to a cold room.

Milk

Milk is an important part of your diet. But in the past it was a source of danger.

Milk is a rich source of nourishment, not just for you, but also for a wide range of bacteria and other microbes. At room temperature, bacteria grow very quickly in milk. They grow more slowly in a refrigerator, but they are not killed by the cold. They are not even killed by freezing.

Microbes can be destroyed by boiling milk for about five minutes, but this also changes the milk completely and destroys some nutrients. Louis Pasteur was one of the great scientists to study microbes. He discovered that the way to kill microbes without altering the milk was to heat milk to about 70°C for a short time and then cool it very quickly. This process is called pasteurisation.

▼ (Picture 3) All cheese is a result of change by fungus. We call it ripening.

Q **Why do we pasteurise milk?**

Summary
- Microbes are responsible for adding textures and flavours to our food.
- Foods that are likely to contain bacteria can be pasteurised easily.

Weblink: www.curriculumvisions.com

Microbes and disease

Since ancient times, microbes have caused widespread disease.

Most diseases occur when the body's defences are overwhelmed by invading germs. This is true for both plants and animals. Sometimes when this happens, great damage can be done. Most diseases are spread by poor hygiene or by sneezing and coughing (Pictures 1, 2 and 3).

Here is the science behind some famous diseases.

Black Death

This is also called the bubonic plague. It has spread through many continents in the past. One of the worst outbreaks was in the 14th century, when it killed a third of the population of Europe.

Bubonic plague is caused by a bacterium carried by the fleas that live on rats. From time to time, an outbreak kills many rats and then fleas look for humans instead. This is when bubonic plague becomes widespread in people.

▶ (Picture 1) Diseases such as the bubonic plague can be transmitted by animals such as rats. Both rats and humans can catch bubonic plague and die.

Potato famine

The cause of the great famine in Ireland in 1844 and 1845 was the failure of the potato crop. This occurred when a fungus spread through the crop, killing many plants. The result was that many people did not have enough to eat and starved or migrated to other countries.

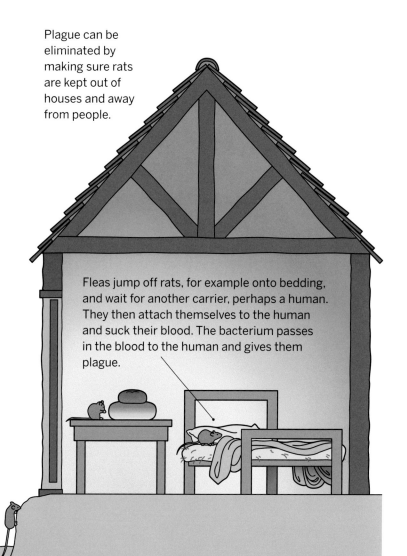

Plague can be eliminated by making sure rats are kept out of houses and away from people.

Fleas jump off rats, for example onto bedding, and wait for another carrier, perhaps a human. They then attach themselves to the human and suck their blood. The bacterium passes in the blood to the human and gives them plague.

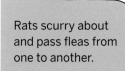

Fleas on rats carry the plague bacteria and can pass it to people if rats and people share the same areas.

Rats scurry about and pass fleas from one to another.

Weblink: www.curriculumvisions.com

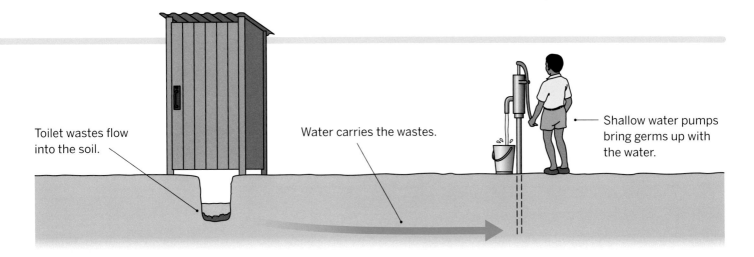

Toilet wastes flow into the soil.

Water carries the wastes.

Shallow water pumps bring germs up with the water.

Influenza epidemic

Influenza is a modern virus that regularly kills thousands, and sometimes millions. For example, between 1918 and 1919 influenza killed more than 20 million people. This was more than died in the four years of World War I.

Malaria

Malaria is a tropical disease caused by a protozoan. Malaria affects millions of people every year. The protozoan lives in the blood. It is carried between animals by a blood-sucking mosquito.

Aids

Aids is caused by a virus that destroys the cells that normally attack invading germs. It is called the human immunodeficiency virus, or HIV. Like many viruses, this virus can change rapidly, making it hard to kill. It does not travel in air or water, but only in human body fluids. The only way to prevent Aids is by making sure that fluids from one infected person are not carried to another.

Q Why should drinking water not be taken from places near to soil toilets?

▲ (Picture 2) Many diseases, such as cholera, are spread in the water supply, especially when liquids from toilets flow into drinking water supplies.

▲ (Picture 3) When somebody has a cold or the flu (influenza), and sneezes or coughs, then some of the viruses that cause the illness are sent out into the air. Their spread is reduced by using a handkerchief.

Summary
• Microbes have been responsible for large numbers of deaths – often called plagues.
• Microbes can be spread by poor hygiene.
• Microbes can also be spread in the air.

Weblink: www.curriculumvisions.com

Staying healthy

Keeping germs at bay is one of the best ways of staying healthy.

There are millions of types of microbes about. Most are harmless, but some may cause disease. If you want to keep these germs away, then science gives you a few simple rules to follow.

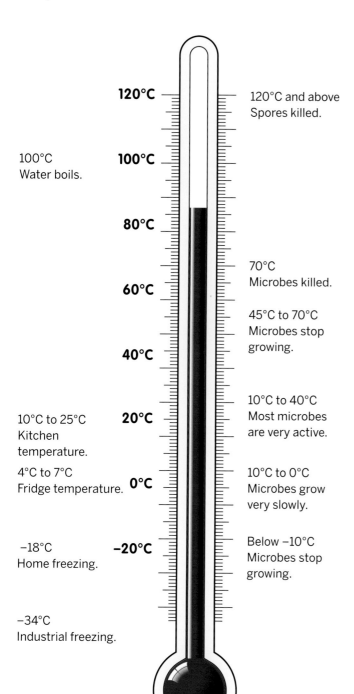

120°C and above
Spores killed.

70°C
Microbes killed.

45°C to 70°C
Microbes stop growing.

10°C to 40°C
Most microbes are very active.

10°C to 0°C
Microbes grow very slowly.

Below −10°C
Microbes stop growing.

120°C

100°C
100°C Water boils.

80°C

60°C

40°C

20°C
10°C to 25°C Kitchen temperature.
4°C to 7°C Fridge temperature.

0°C

−18°C Home freezing.
−20°C

−34°C Industrial freezing.

Store food safely

Most of the time when food smells bad and goes rotten, it is because of the growth of fungi. But the great majority of food poisoning cases are caused by bacteria. In part this is because food infected by bacteria may not look, taste or smell bad.

The bacteria that cause the most trouble are called salmonella. They often get into the food from the hands of people who have been to the toilet and then not washed their hands, or from the feet of flies that have settled on human waste and then on food.

Even those bacteria that cause food poisoning are only harmful in large numbers. Warm conditions allow bacteria to grow quickly (Picture 1). Food-poisoning bacteria will not grow and multiply quickly if the temperature is below 7°C. This is why refrigerators should be set below this temperature. So, if cooked meat is left out in a warm room for many hours it will be much more dangerous to eat than the same food kept in a refrigerator.

◀ **(Picture 1) This diagram shows the temperatures that are needed to stop microbes from growing quickly. A refrigerator only slows them down. A freezer stops them growing almost entirely because it is so much colder. Notice that at high temperatures (for example in an oven) all microbes are destroyed, which is one reason why we cook foods.**

▲ (Picture 2) Chlorine is added to tap water and swimming pool water to act as a disinfectant and kill germs.

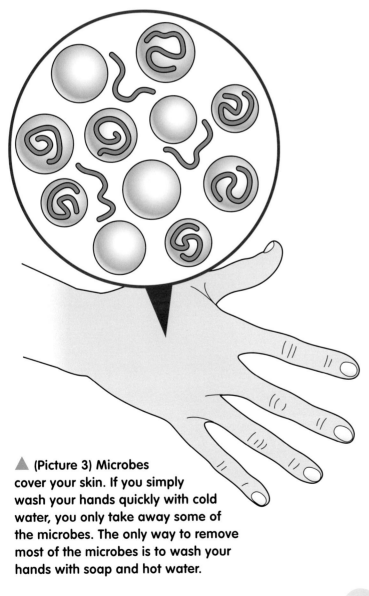

▲ (Picture 3) Microbes cover your skin. If you simply wash your hands quickly with cold water, you only take away some of the microbes. The only way to remove most of the microbes is to wash your hands with soap and hot water.

Don't spread germs

Using a disinfectant kills germs (Picture 2), and so does thorough cooking.

Bacteria can also get onto food from hands (Picture 3). Washing your hands with soap and water loosens the bacteria's grip on your skin, and allows them to be washed away. Rinsing with water alone does not loosen all germs.

You can also pick up germs from objects, such as doorknobs and stair railings, touched by other people who aren't good handwashers.

So always wash your hands:

▶ Before putting your fingers in your mouth or rubbing your eyes.
▶ Before treating a wound.
▶ Before handling food – even your packed lunch or snack.
▶ After you have been to the toilet.
▶ After you have handled raw meat.
▶ After you handle rubbish.
▶ After you handle a pet.
▶ After you help someone who is ill.

 Why should we wash our hands with soap and water?

Summary
• Cool conditions stop the growth of bacteria on food.
• Store raw foods away from cooked foods.
• Always heat food to above 75°C.
• Wash hands with soap and water.
• Keep flies off food.

21

Are microbes good or bad?

There are far more good microbes than bad ones, so we need to encourage the good ones and keep out the bad ones.

As you have seen, some microbes do immense good, while others do immense harm. Because a few microbes cause very serious illness (such as food poisoning and Aids), some people think that we should try to sterilise everything and wipe out all of the microbes. Would this be wise?

In fact it would be a disaster. This is because many microbes are vital to life on Earth. In fact we would die without them!

Here are some of the useful microbes and what they do:

Fungi and bacteria can be used to produce powerful antibiotics such as penicillin and tetracycline. These can be used to fight the germs that cause sore throats, ear infections, diarrhoea and fever.

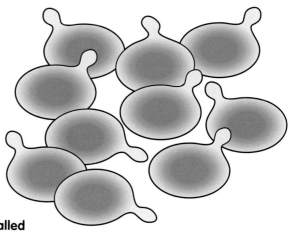

A fungus called 'baker's yeast' makes dough rise. Bread is flat and tougher without it.

A bacterium called Lactobacillus turns milk into yoghurt (look for it on live yoghurt carton labels as part of your healthy diet).

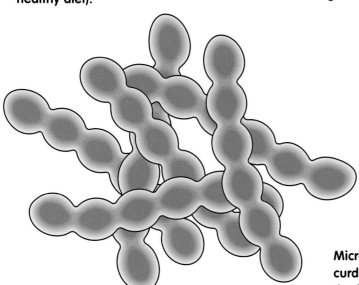

A microbe called Pseudomonas cleans up our sewage waste for free.

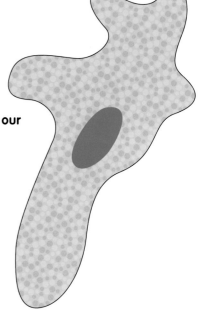

Microbes make milk curdle and bring out the flavour in cheese.

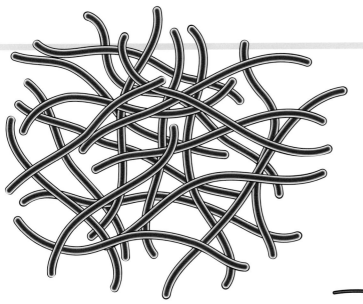

A fungus called Arbuscular helps crops take up nutrients from the soil.

A bacterium called E. coli lives in your lower gut and helps you to digest your food.

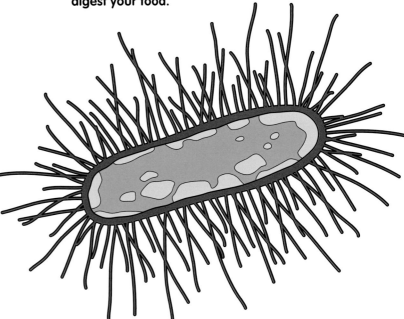

A bacterium in the soil called 'Bt' is a natural pest killer.

Except for viruses (which are always harmful), a microbe is usually only bad when it gets in the wrong place. For example, E. coli is fine when it is deep down in your gut, but if you eat it with contaminated food, it gets into the wrong place in the body and causes illness.

Bacteria produce special chemicals called enzymes. We use enzymes to make soy sauce, soda, beer, wine, cheese, chewing gum, to clean our washing (called biological action), to give the stone-washed look on blue jeans, and for many other useful things.

So you don't want to get rid of microbes, you simply want to keep them in their right places.

For microbe buffs:

Arbuscular = Arbuscular mycorrhizas
Baker's yeast = Saccharomyces cerevisiae
Bt = Bacillus thuringiensis
E. coli = Escherichia coli
Fungus that produced the first penicillin = Penicillium notatum
Lactobacillus in yoghurt = Lactobacillus acidophilus and Lactobacillus bulgaricus

Summary

- Most microbes are vital to life.
- Microbes only become dangerous when they get into the wrong part of your body.
- Only viruses are always harmful.

Weblink: www.curriculumvisions.com

Index

Curriculum Visions

Science@School

Teacher's Guide

There is a Teacher's Guide to accompany this book, available only from the publisher.

There's much more online including videos

You will find multimedia resources covering this and ALL 37 QCA Key Stage 1 and 2 science units as well as history, geography, religion, MFL, maths, music, spelling and more at:

www.CurriculumVisions.com

(Subscription required)

A CVP Book
This second edition © Atlantic Europe Publishing 2011

First edition 2002. First reprint 2004. Second reprint 2006.

The right of Brian Knapp to be identified as the author of this work has been asserted by him in accordance with the Copyright, Designs and Patents Act 1988.

All rights reserved. No part of this publication may be reproduced, stored in a retrieval system, or transmitted in any form or by any means, electronic, mechanical, photocopying, recording or otherwise, without prior permission of the copyright holder.

Author
Brian Knapp, BSc, PhD

Educational Consultant
Peter Riley, BSc, C Biol, MI Biol, PGCE

Medical Consultant
Andrew Burnett, MB.ChB, MRCGP, DRCOG

Art Director
Duncan McCrae, BSc

Senior Designer
Adele Humphries, BA, PGCE

Editor
Lisa Magloff, MA

Illustrations
David Woodroffe

Designed and produced by
Atlantic Europe Publishing

Printed in China by
WKT Company Ltd

Volume 6B *Microbes 2nd Edition*
– Curriculum Visions Science@School
A CIP record for this book is available from the British Library.

Paperback ISBN 978 1 86214 679 2

Picture credits
All photographs are from the Earthscape Picture Library

This product is manufactured from sustainable managed forests. For every tree cut down at least one more is planted.